Peggy Parrish
teacuplady53@blogspot.com
Cover pictures by Peggy Parrish
Inside artwork by Peggy Parrish

ISBN-13 978-1542366762

ISBN-10 1542366763

Printed in the United States of America

Welcome to the beauty of Letter D

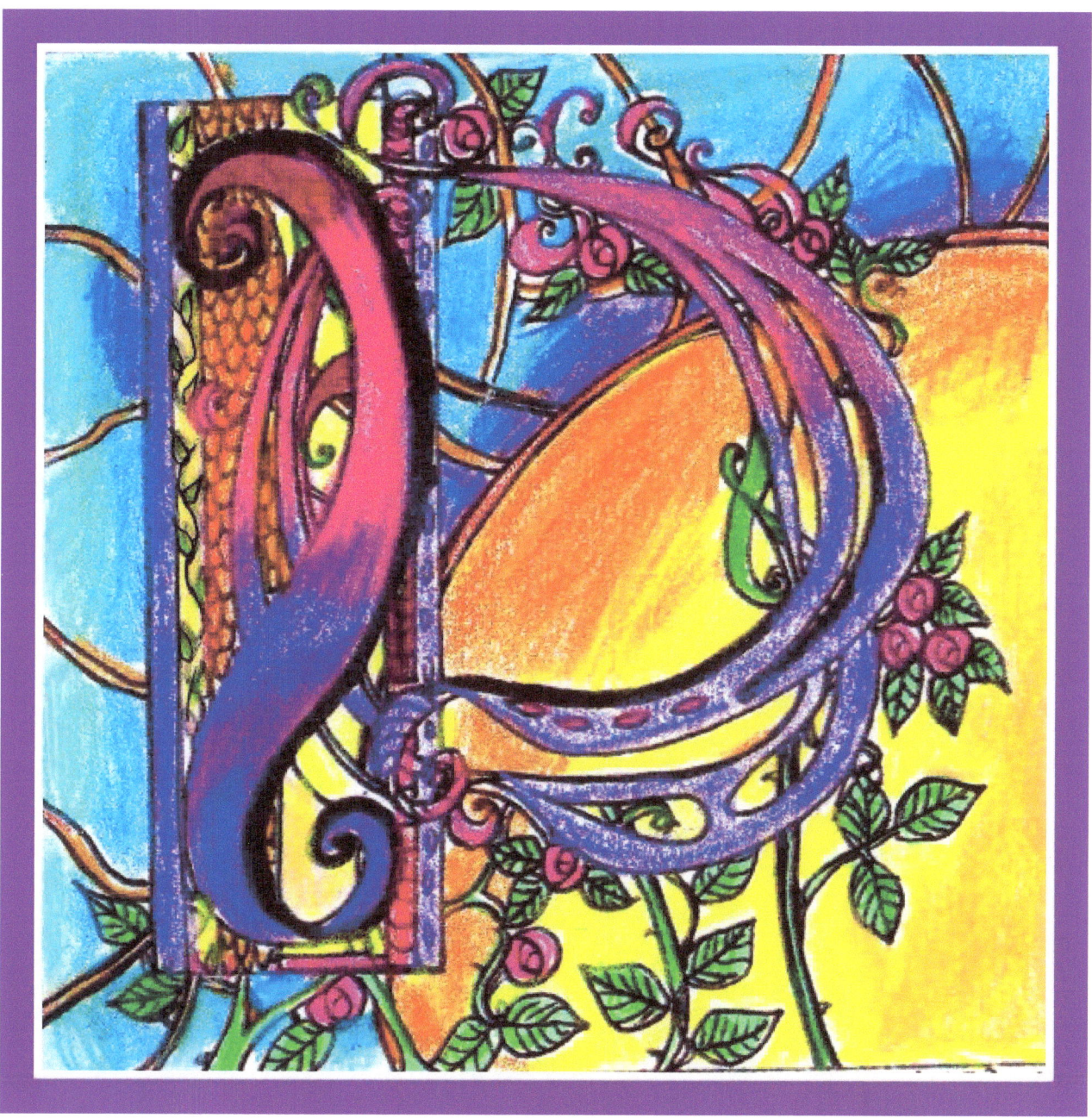

Letter D can have a background

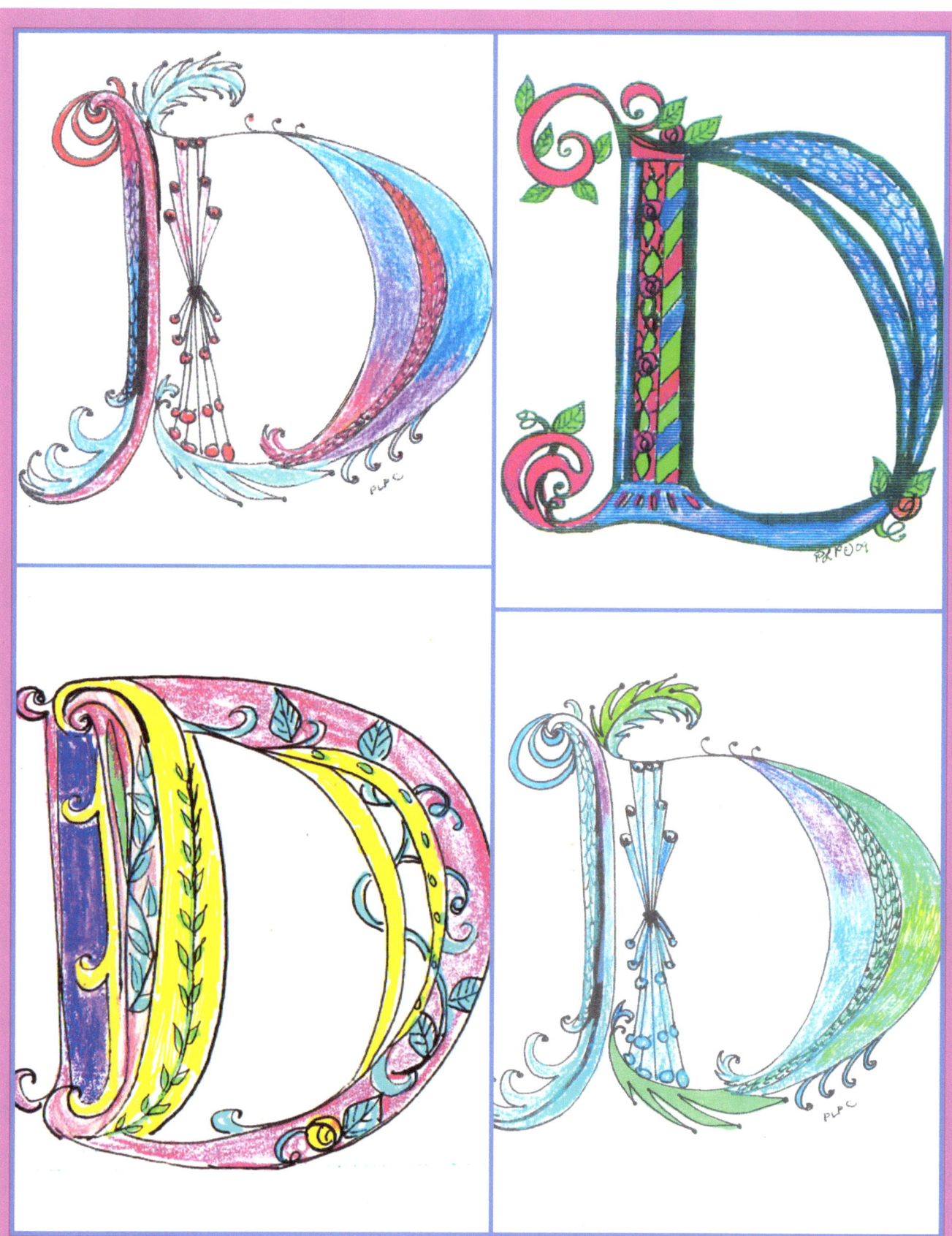

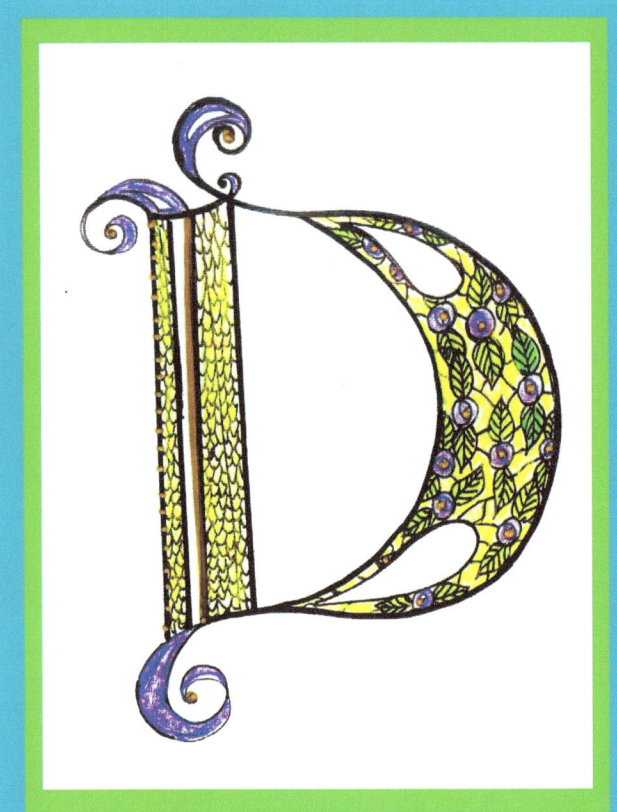
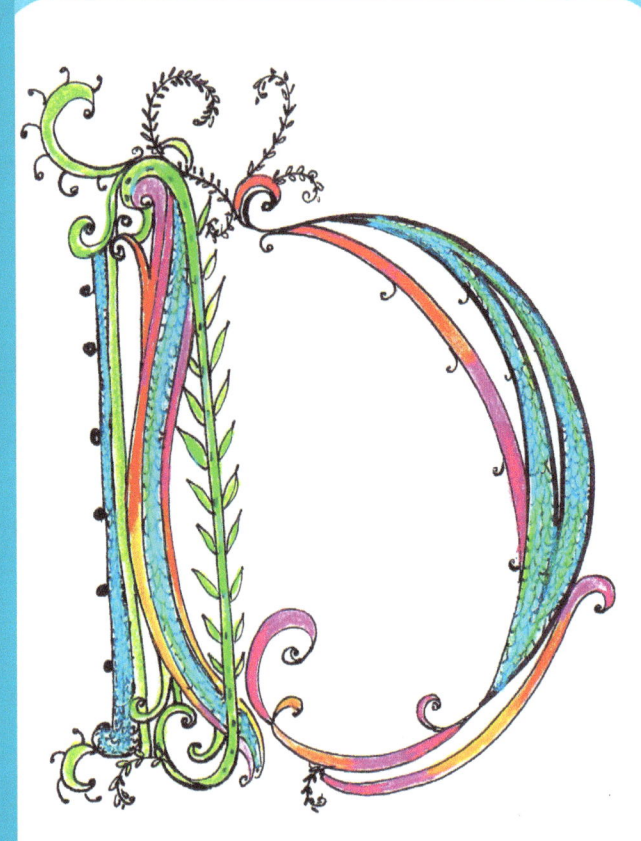
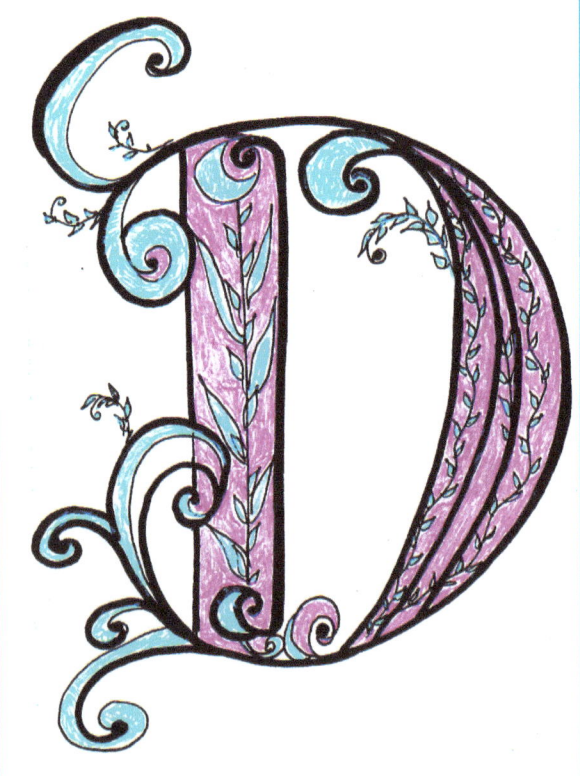
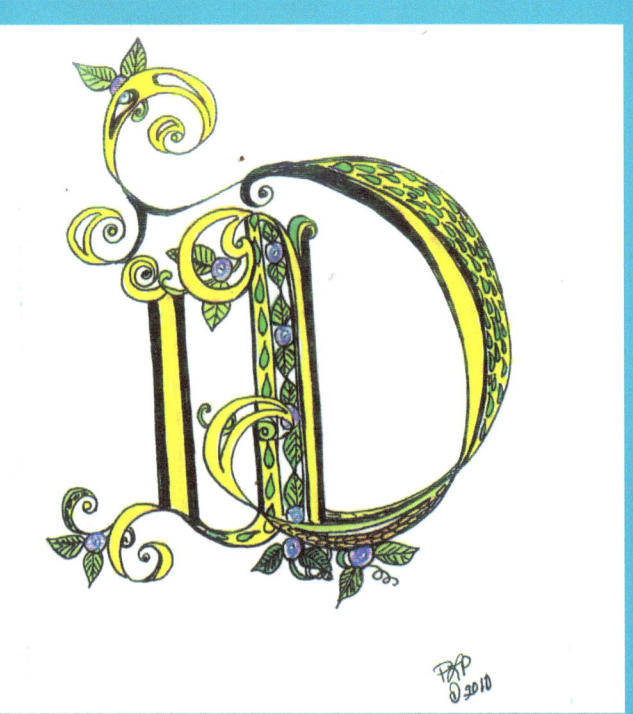

Coloring Tips on Letter D

Here you will find an adventure with the letter D. Uniquely designed letter Ds fill this book. They are waiting for you to color them.

The artist Peggy Louise Parrish is publishing one letter at a time in books for your coloring enjoyment. There are several colored examples within the pages to give you a Gallery of possibilities. Use your imagination and find your own amazing combinations. This book challenges those who enjoy coloring therapy with an opportunity to either copy the artist's way of coloring or choose their own way.

Perhaps your first or last name starts with the letter D. The artist gives permission to those buying this book to make a few "in house" extra copies of the letters you want to color in several ways. Maybe you would like to try multiple ways of coloring your initial D. As long as you leave the artist's initials on the bottom of the design feel free to make a lasting print of your colored copy.

Whether your favorite medium is colored pencils, watercolor pencils, glitter pens, markers or crayons, place a scrap paper under each page while you are working on your letters. If you want letters other than D be patient, the other books are available or in process.

The Delightful Letter D Coloring Book

Waiting to be colored by you

By Peggy Louise Parrish

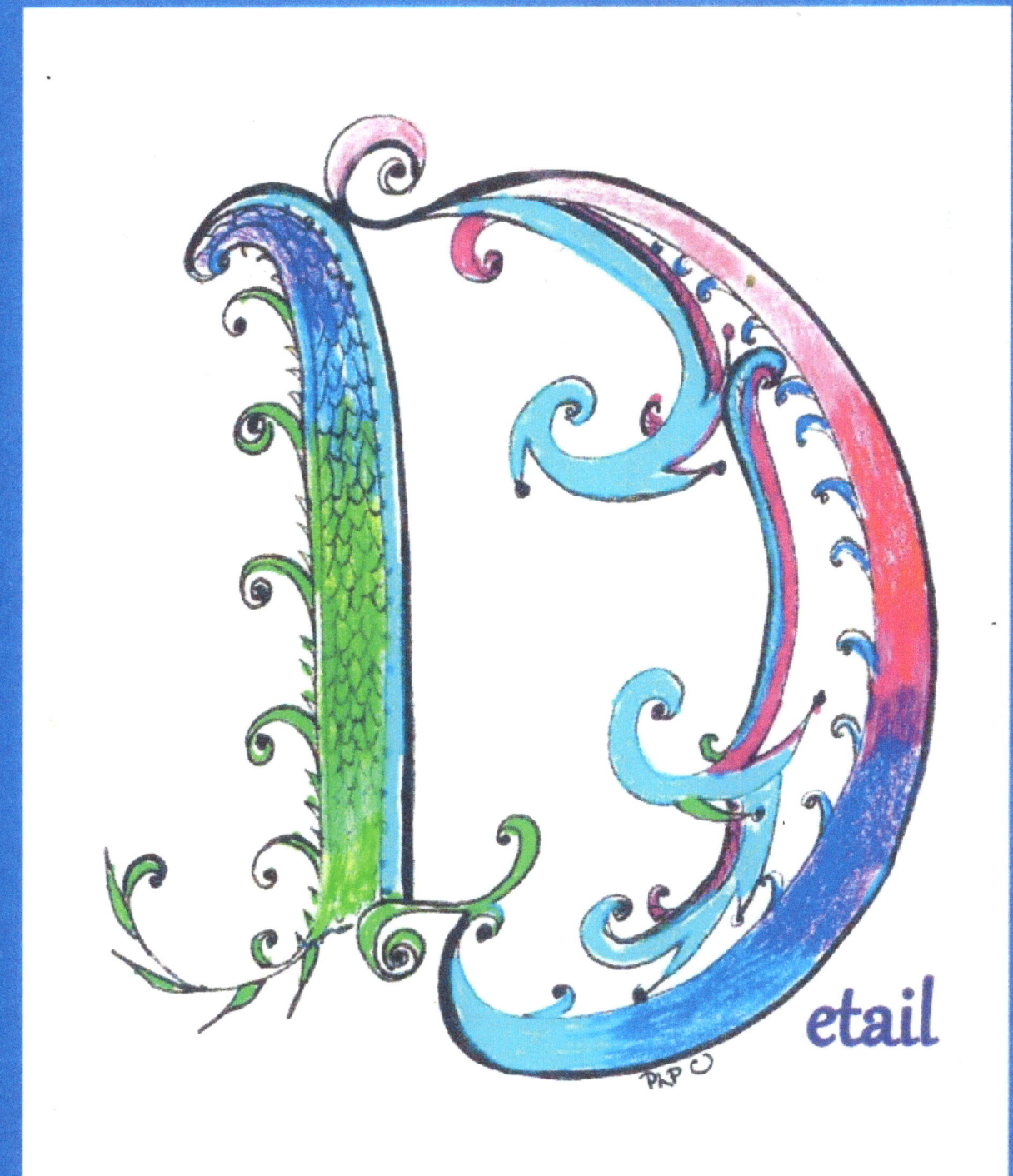

etail

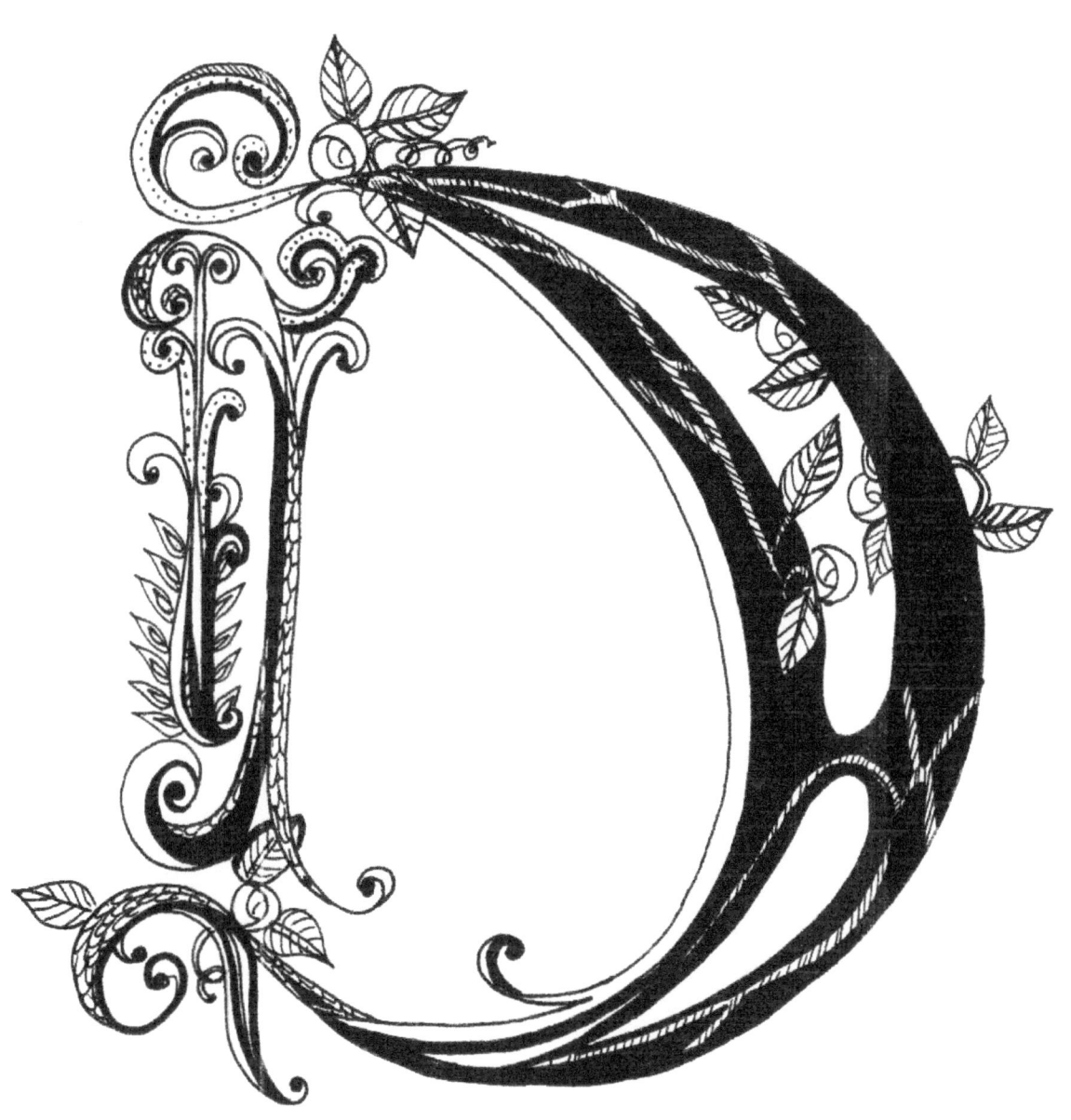

11

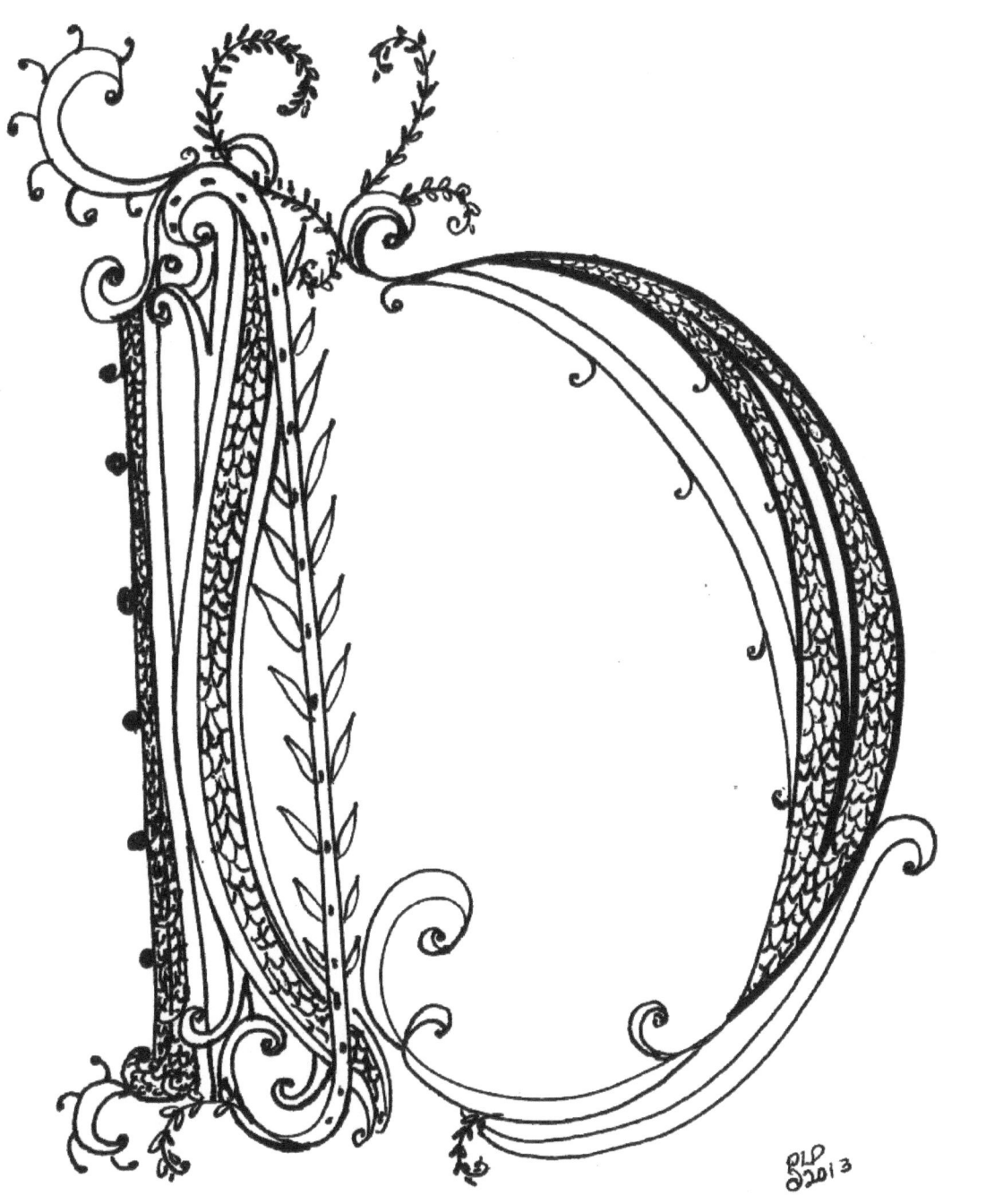

13

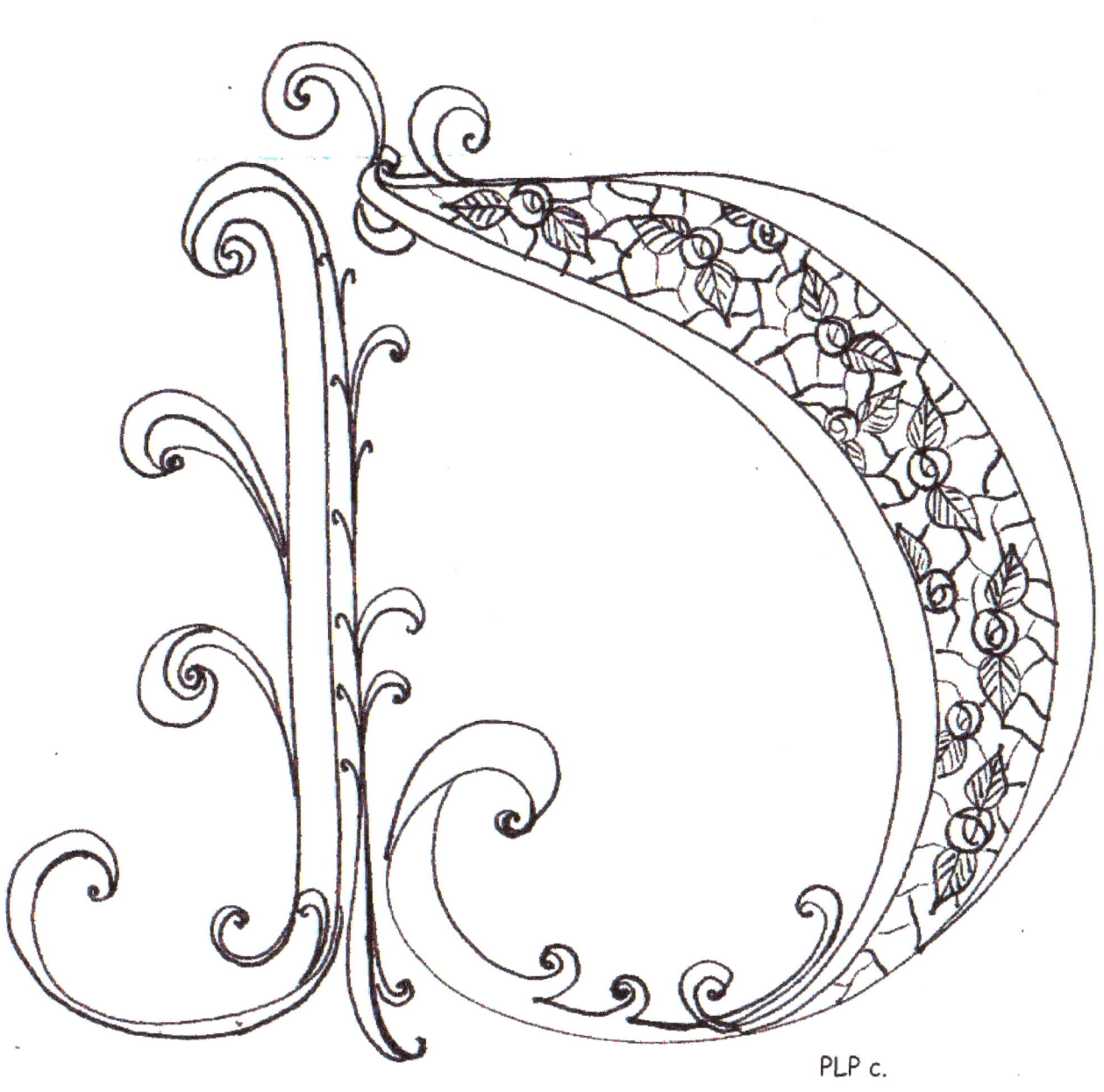

PLP c.

15

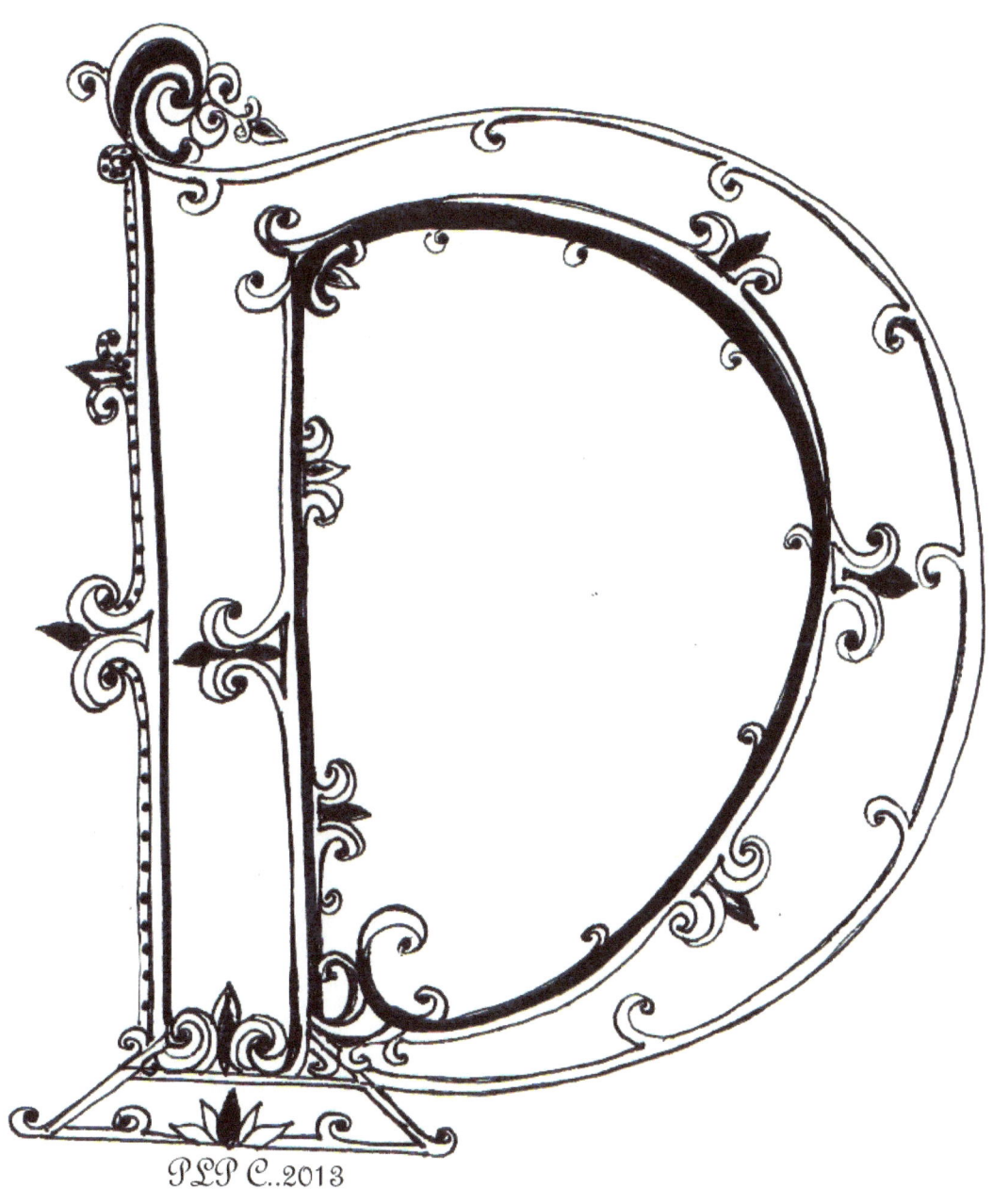

PLP C..2013

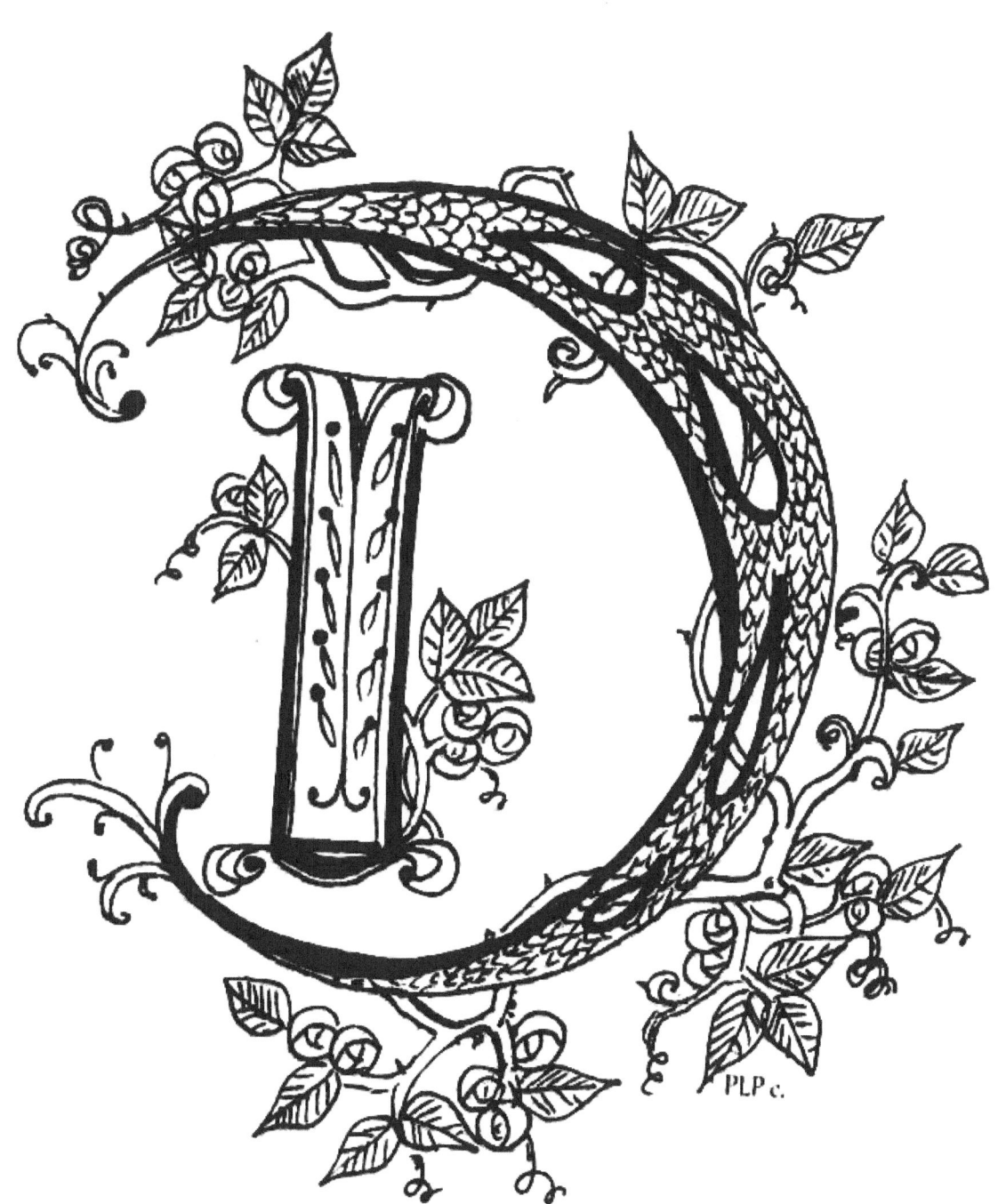

PLP c.

21

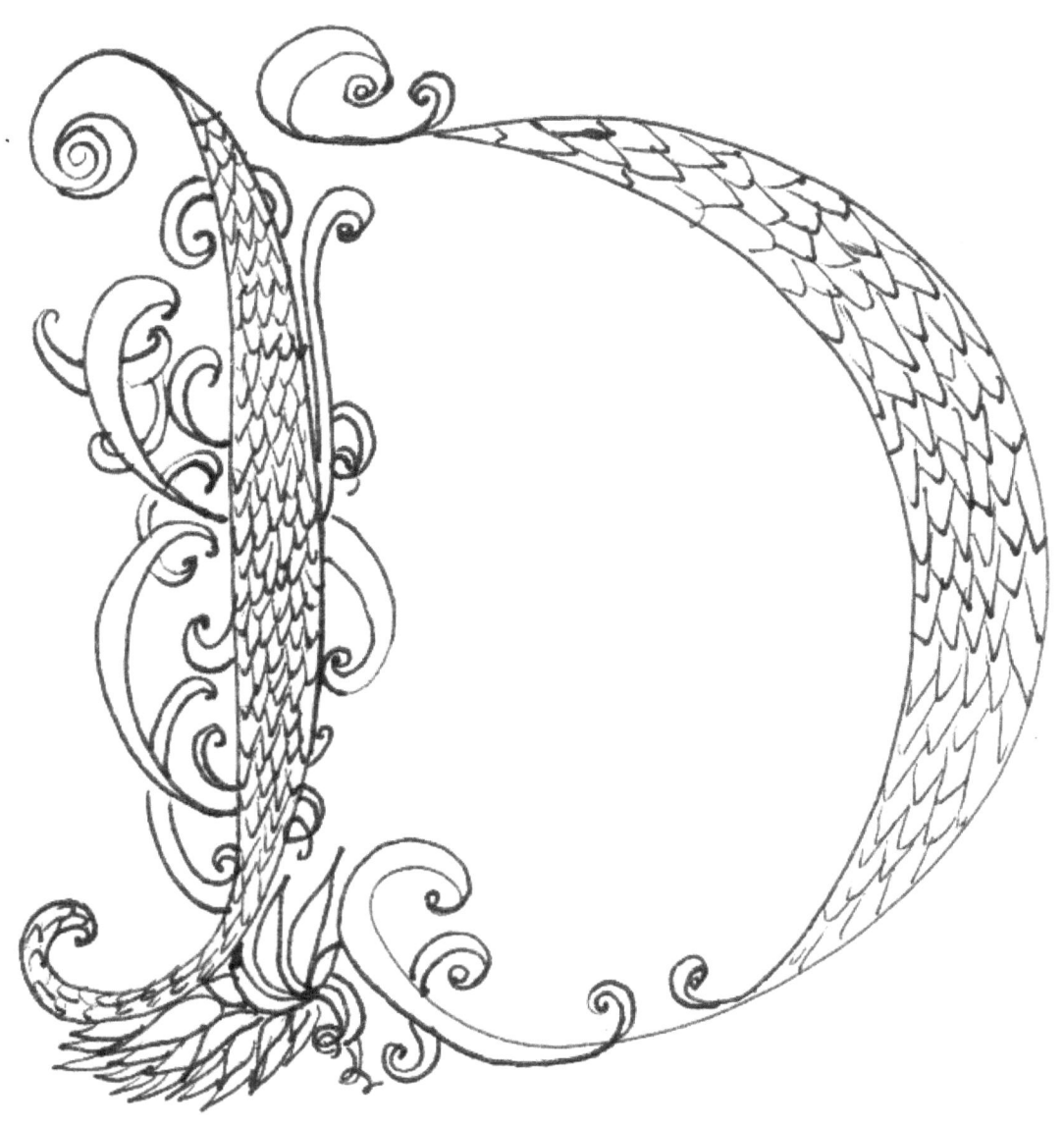

PLP C. 2014

PLP c.

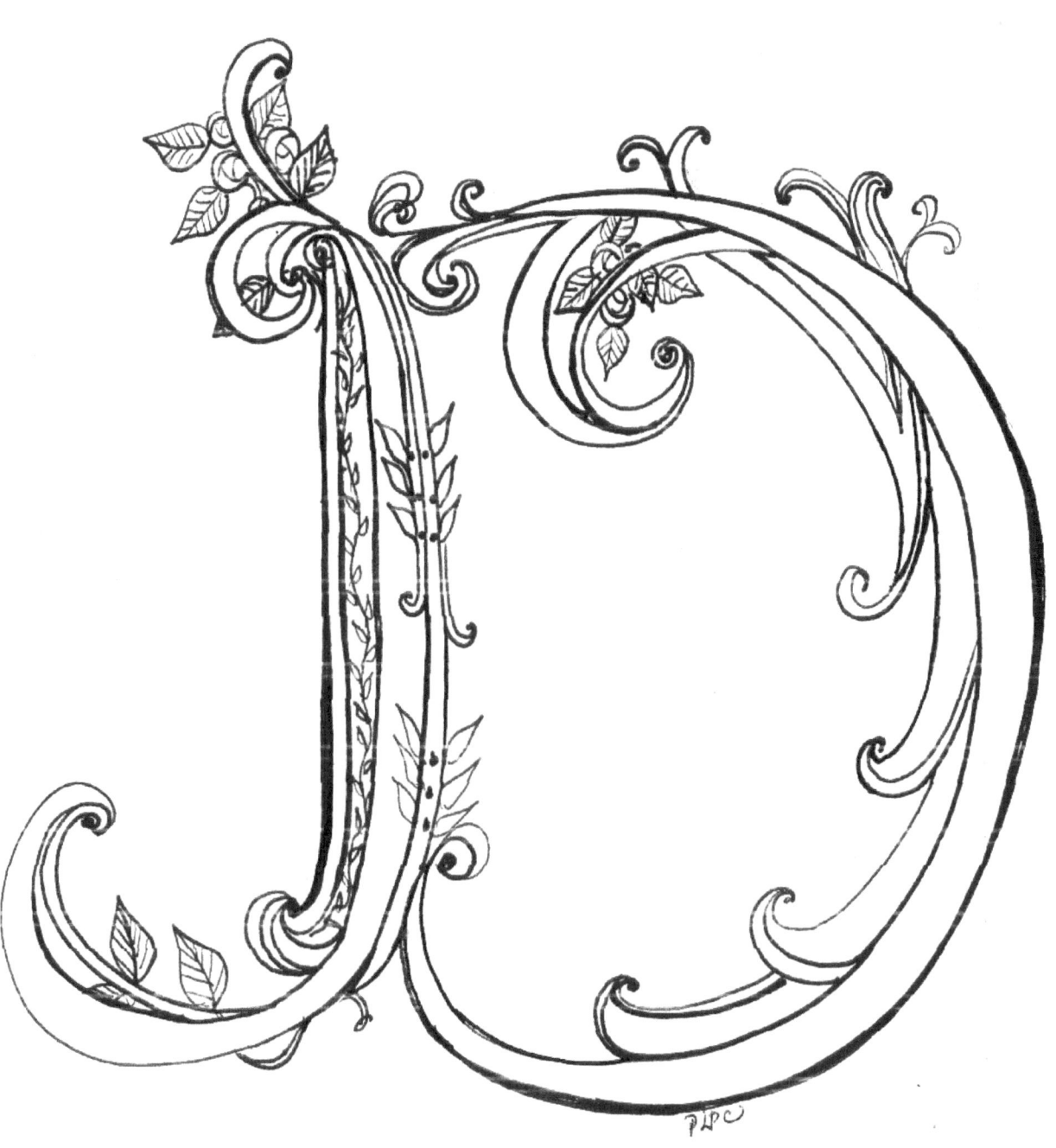

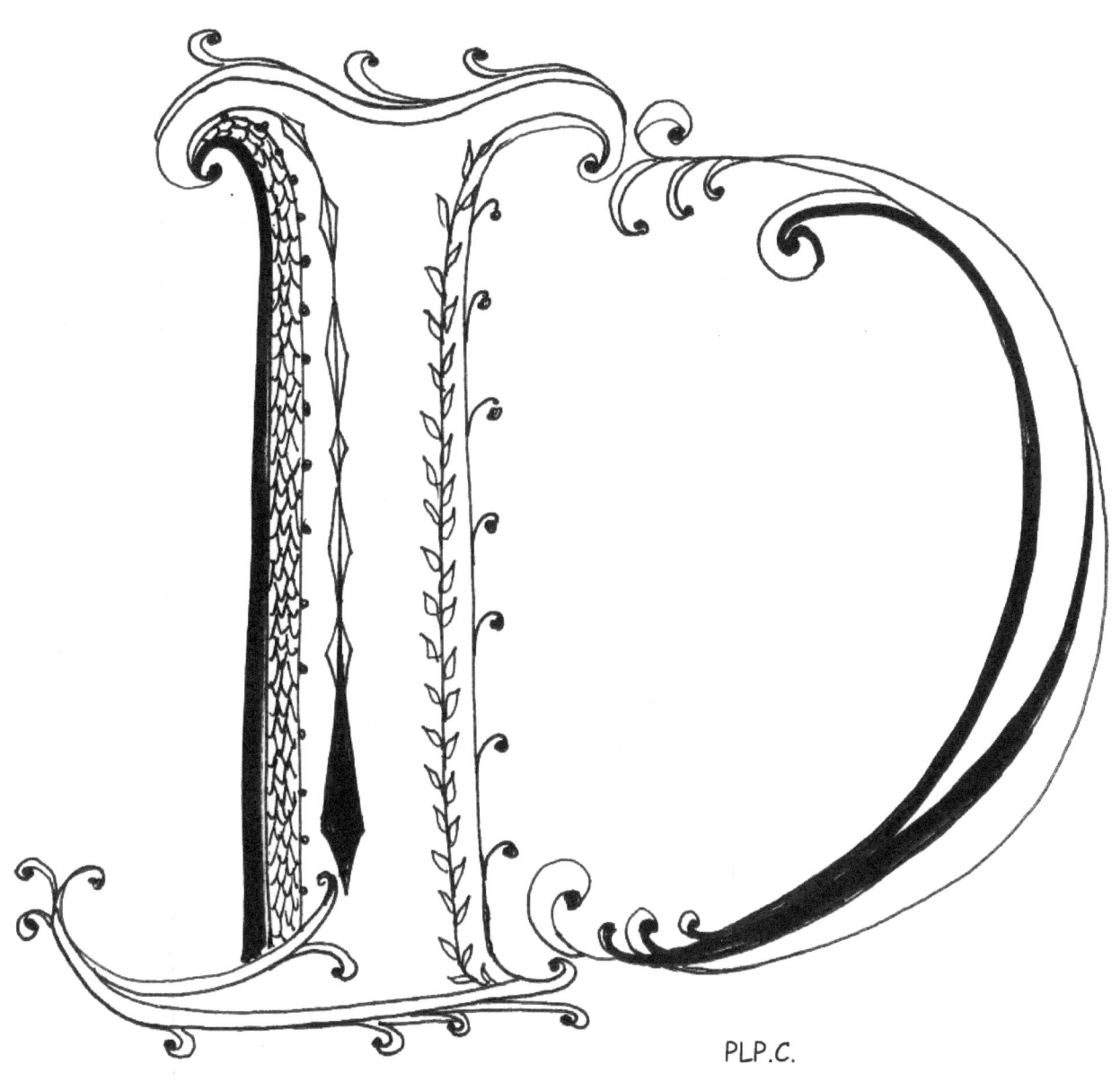

PLP.C.

29

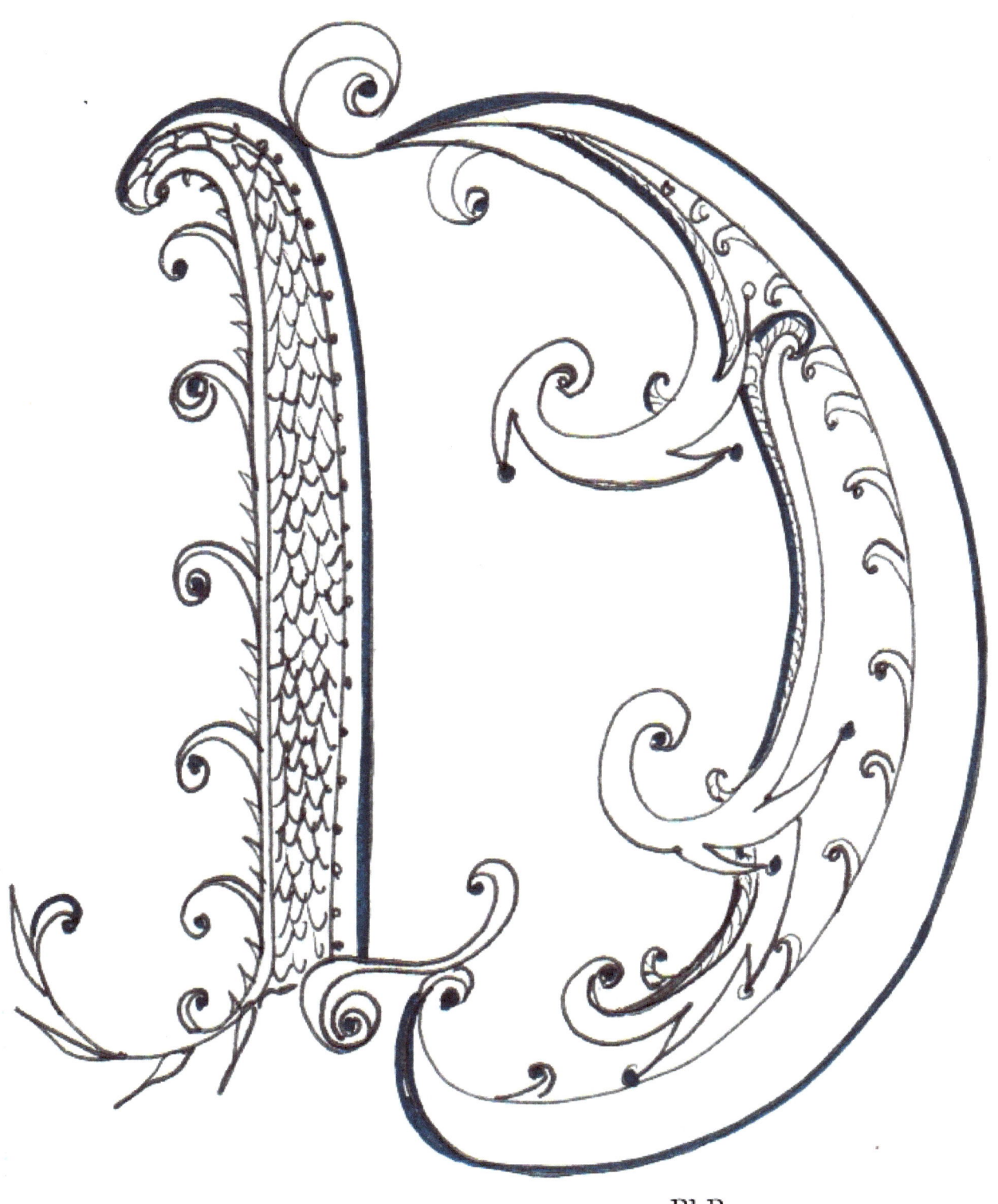

PLP c.

31

PLP C. 2015

33

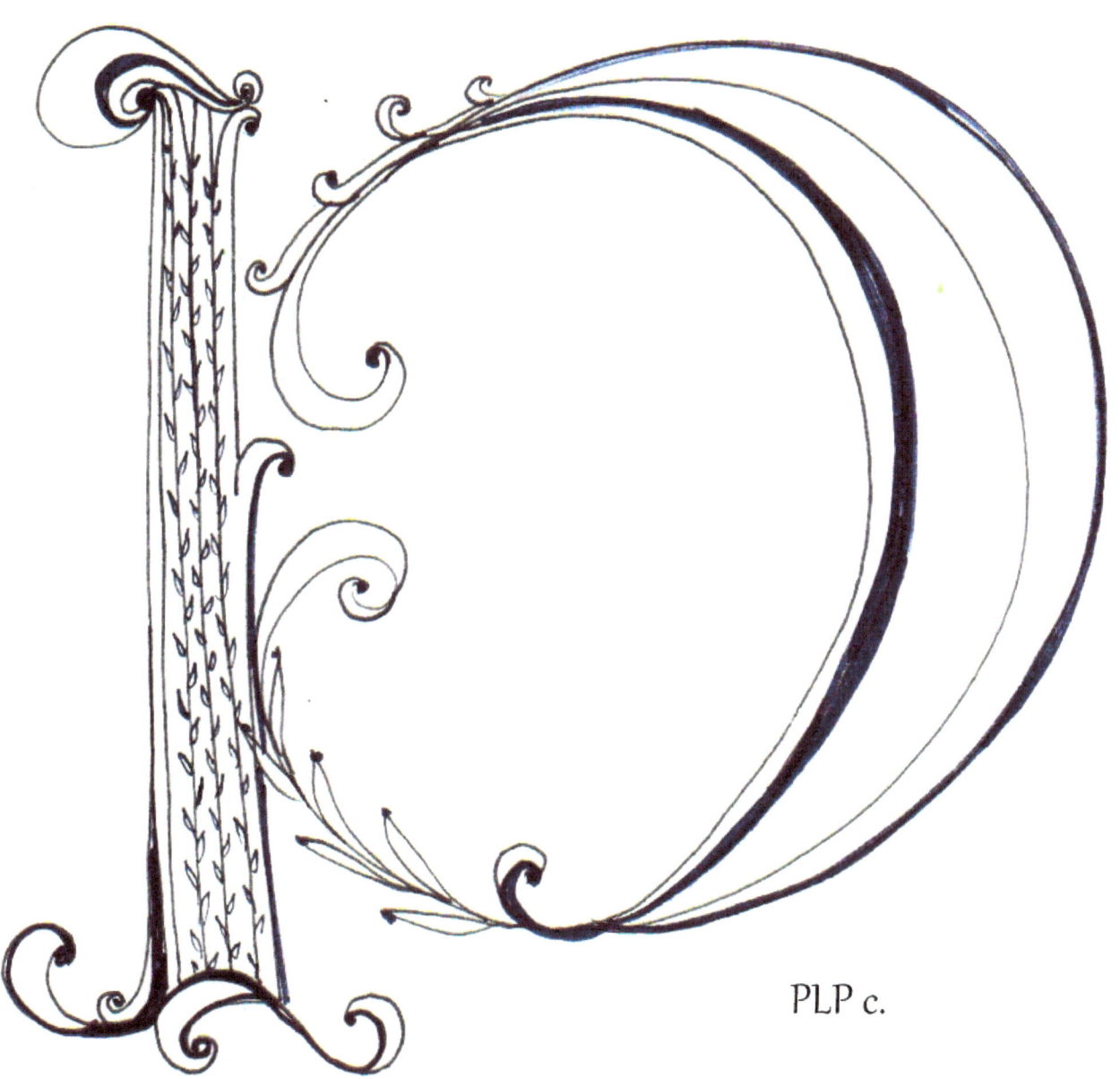

PLP c.

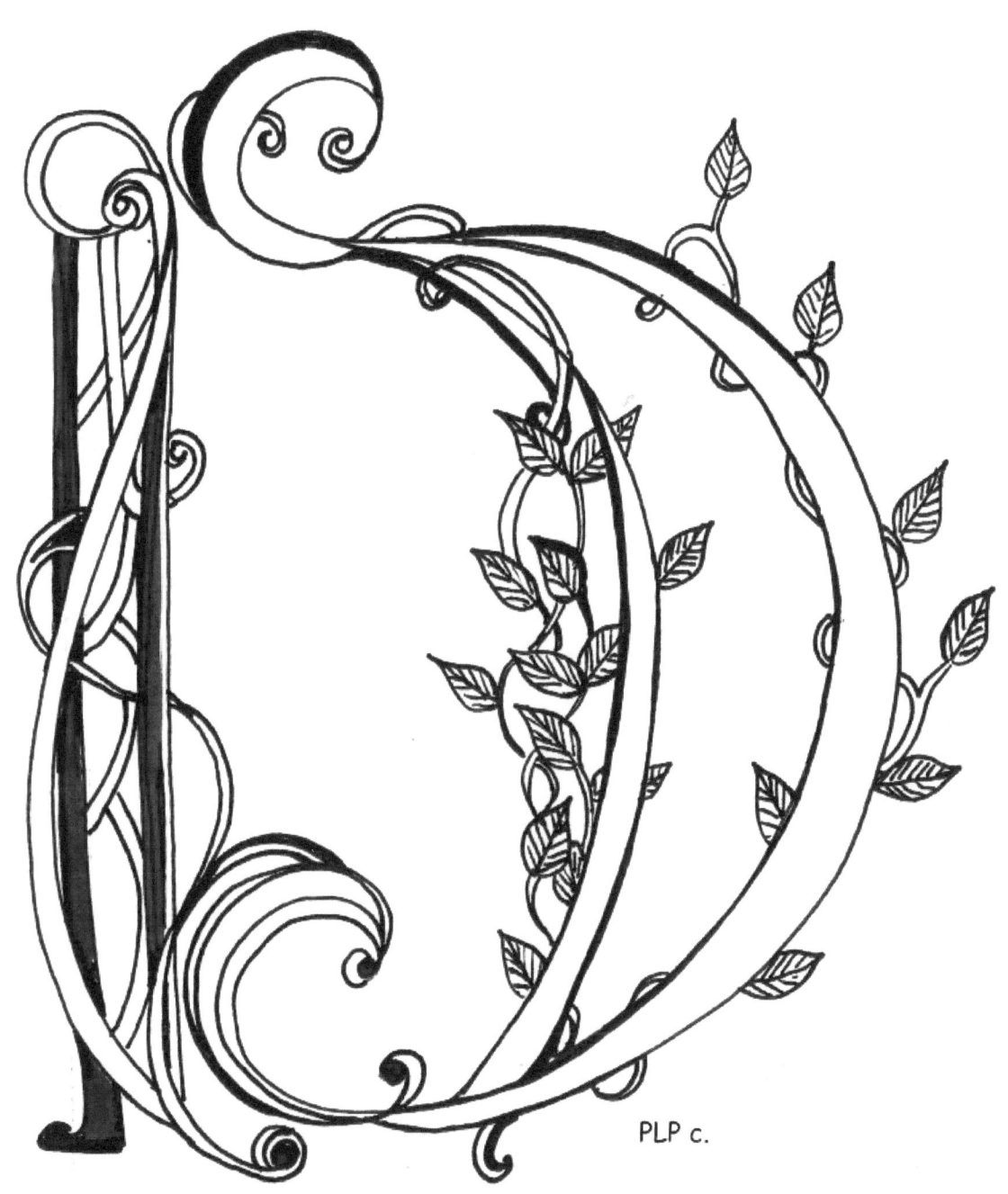

PLP c.

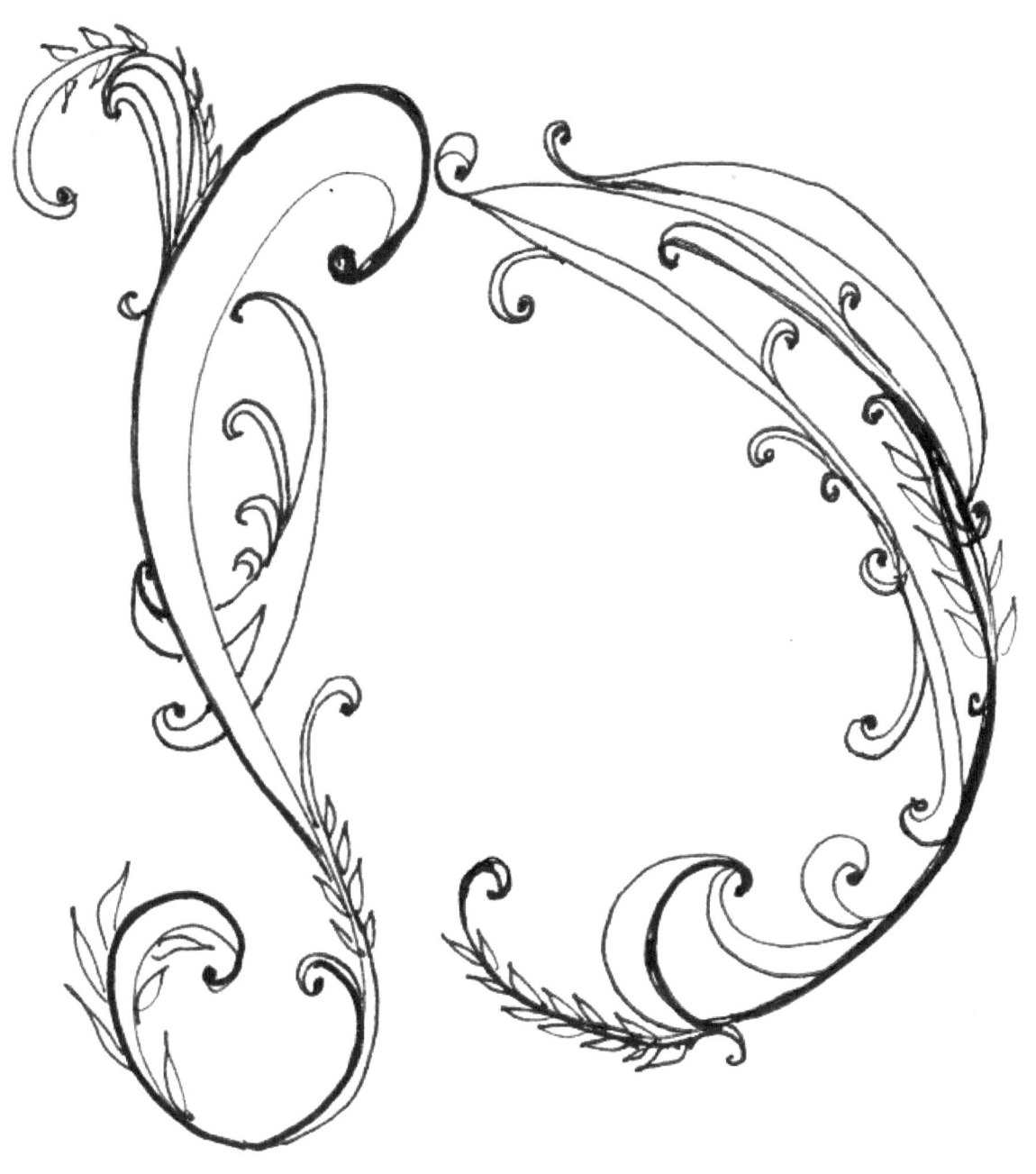

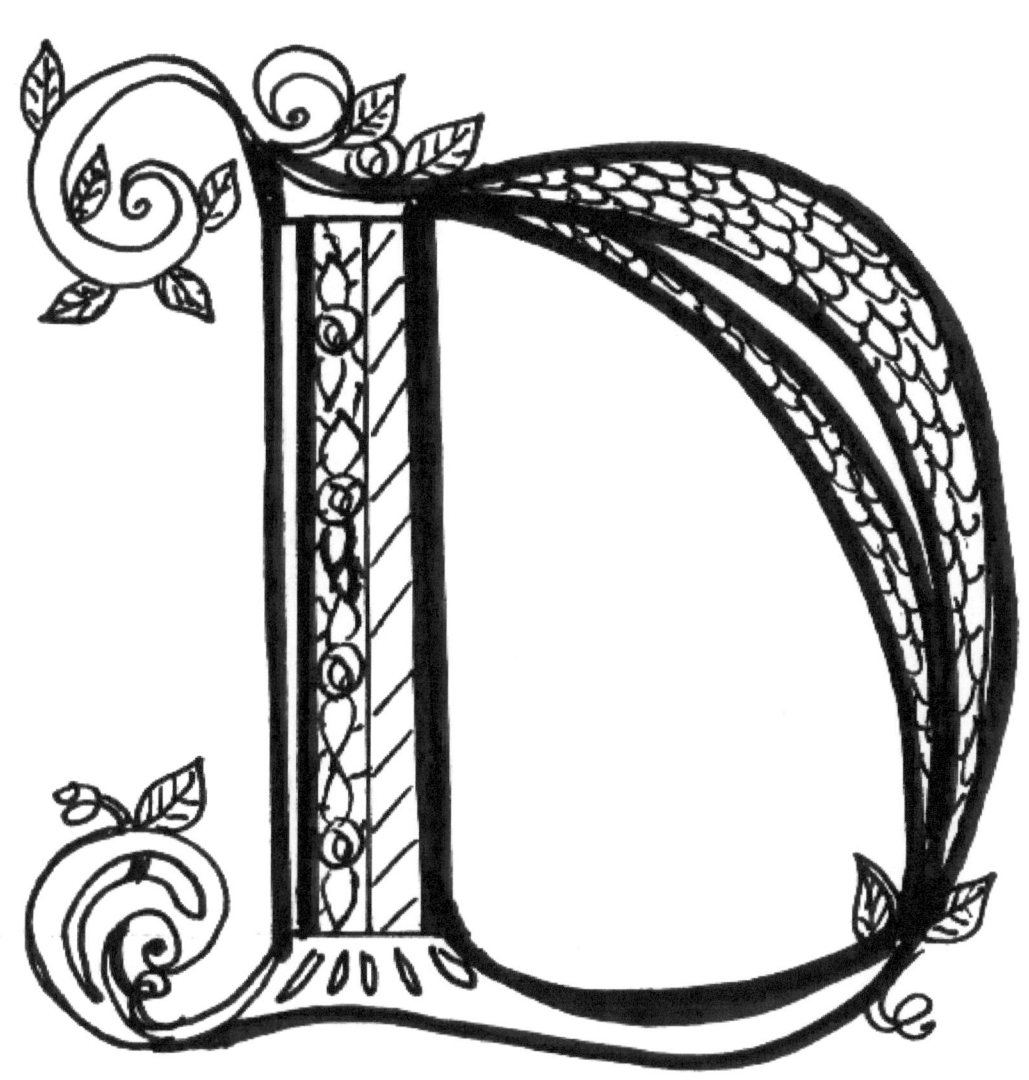

43

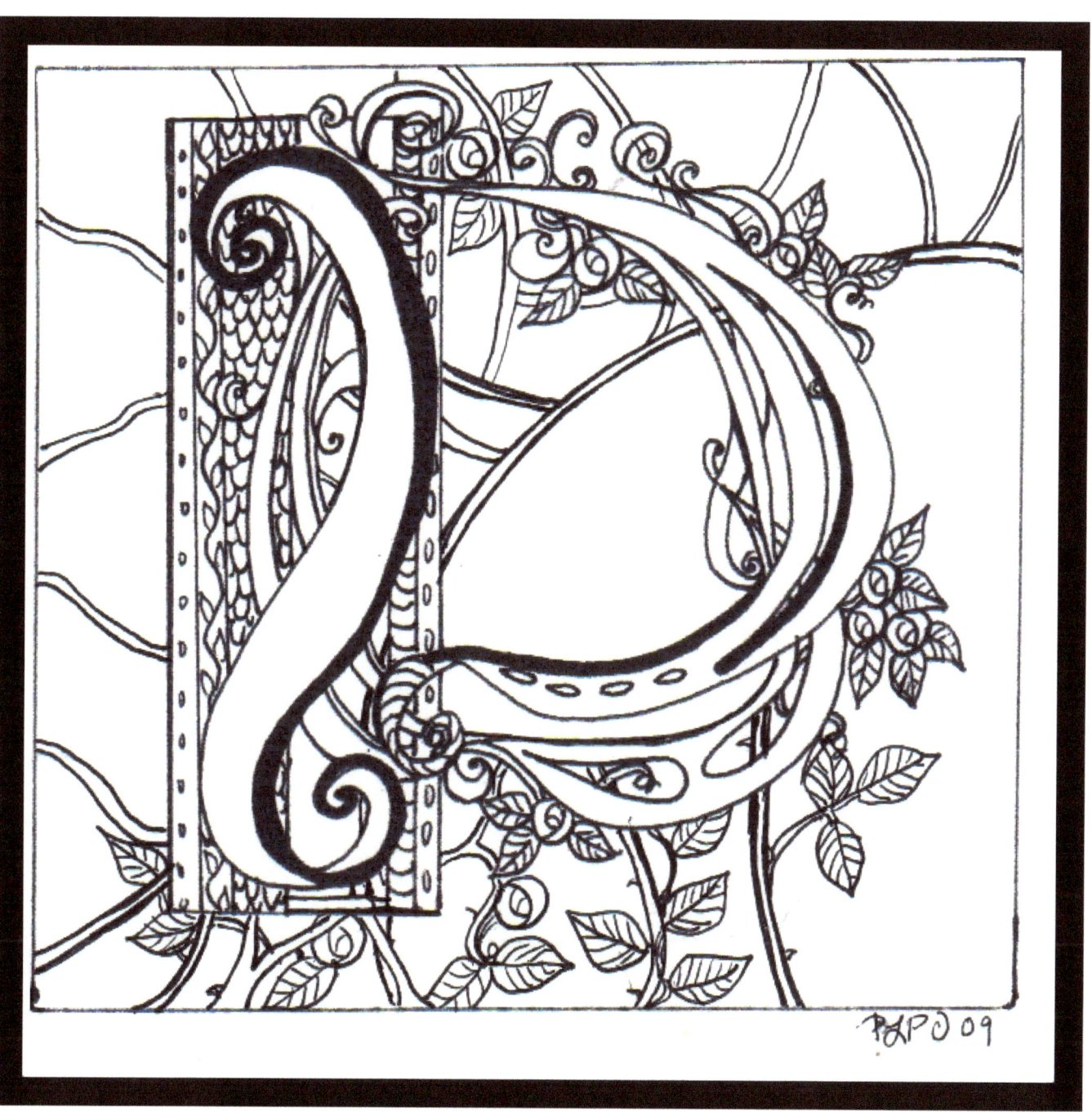

45

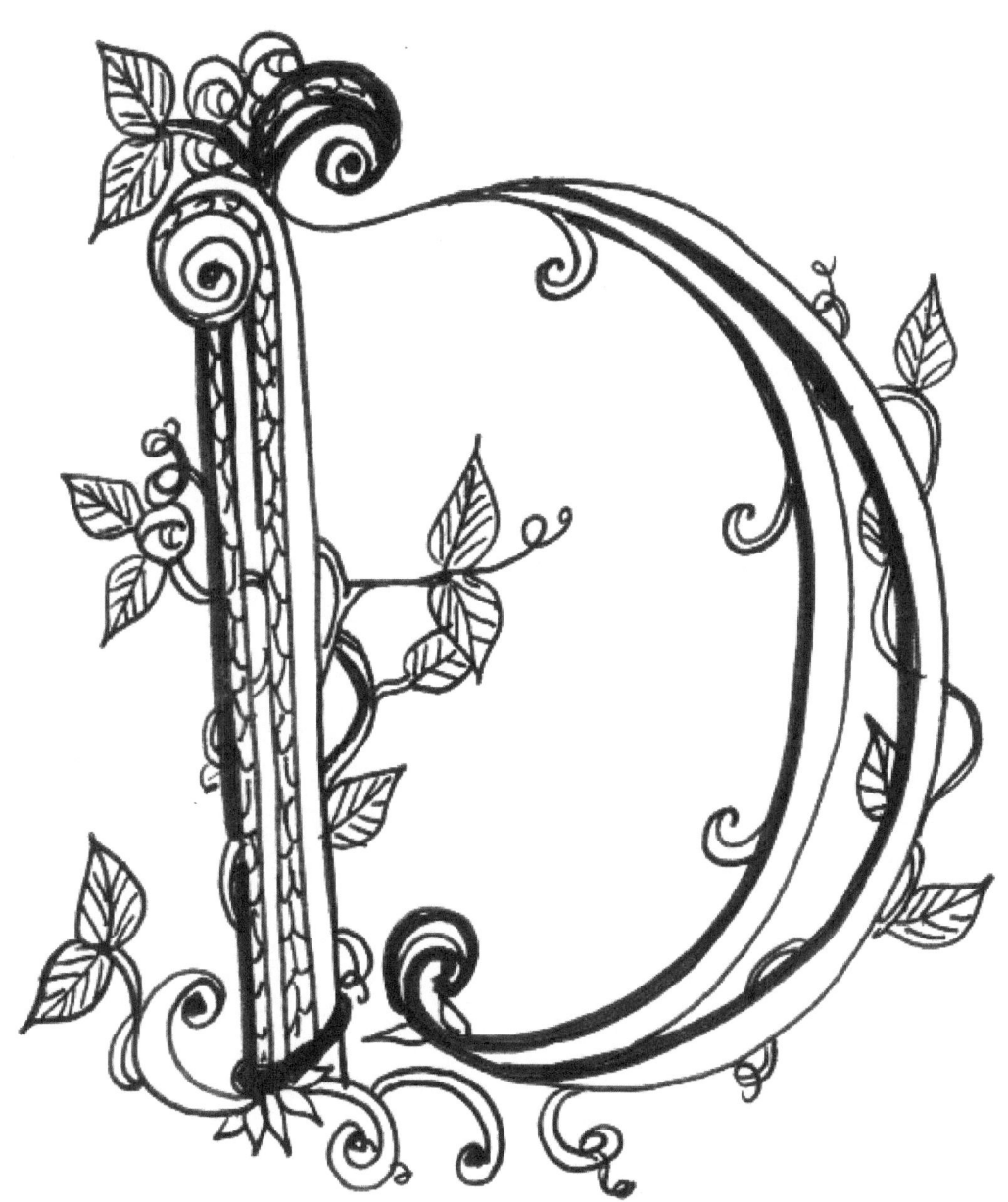

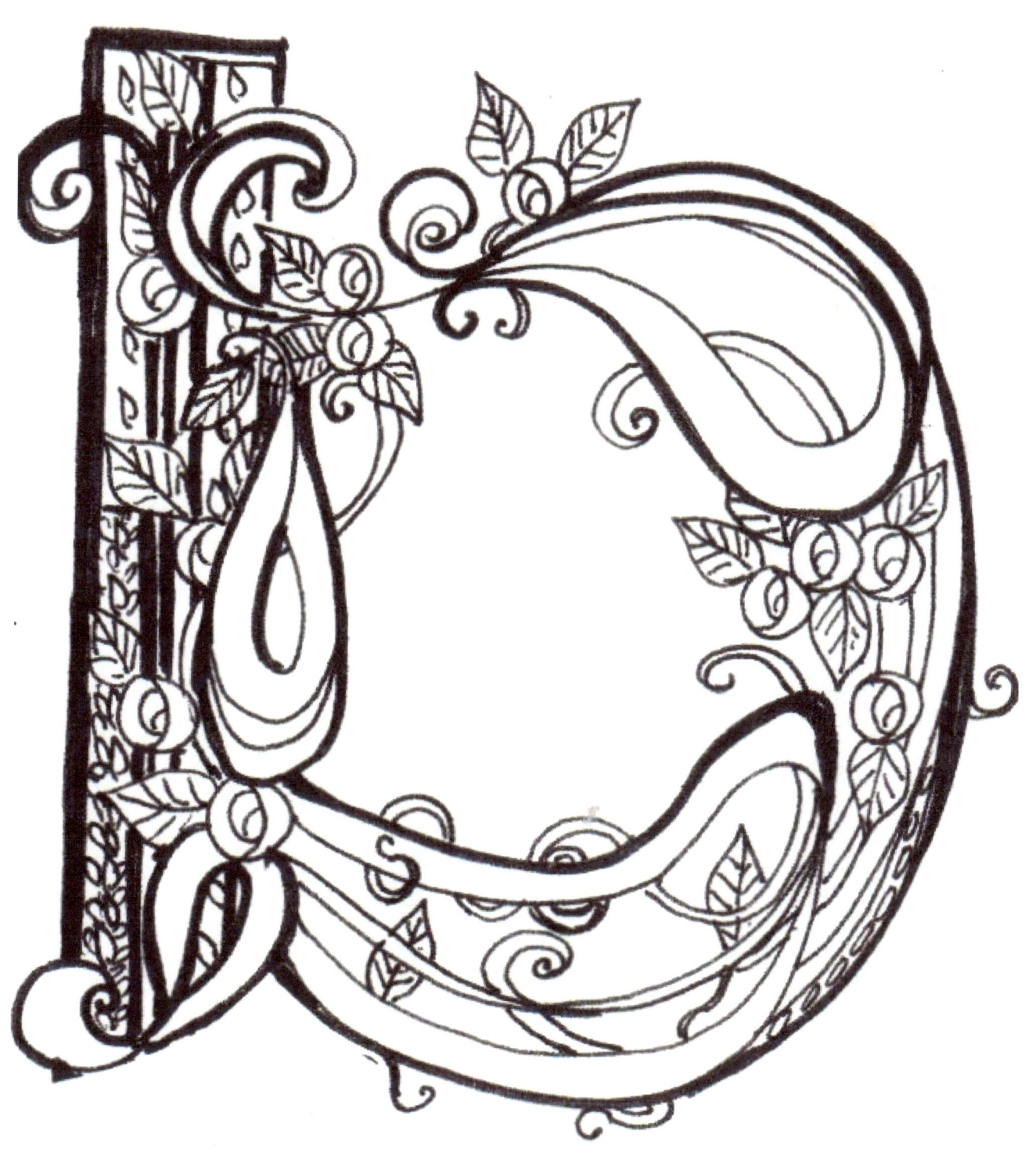

49

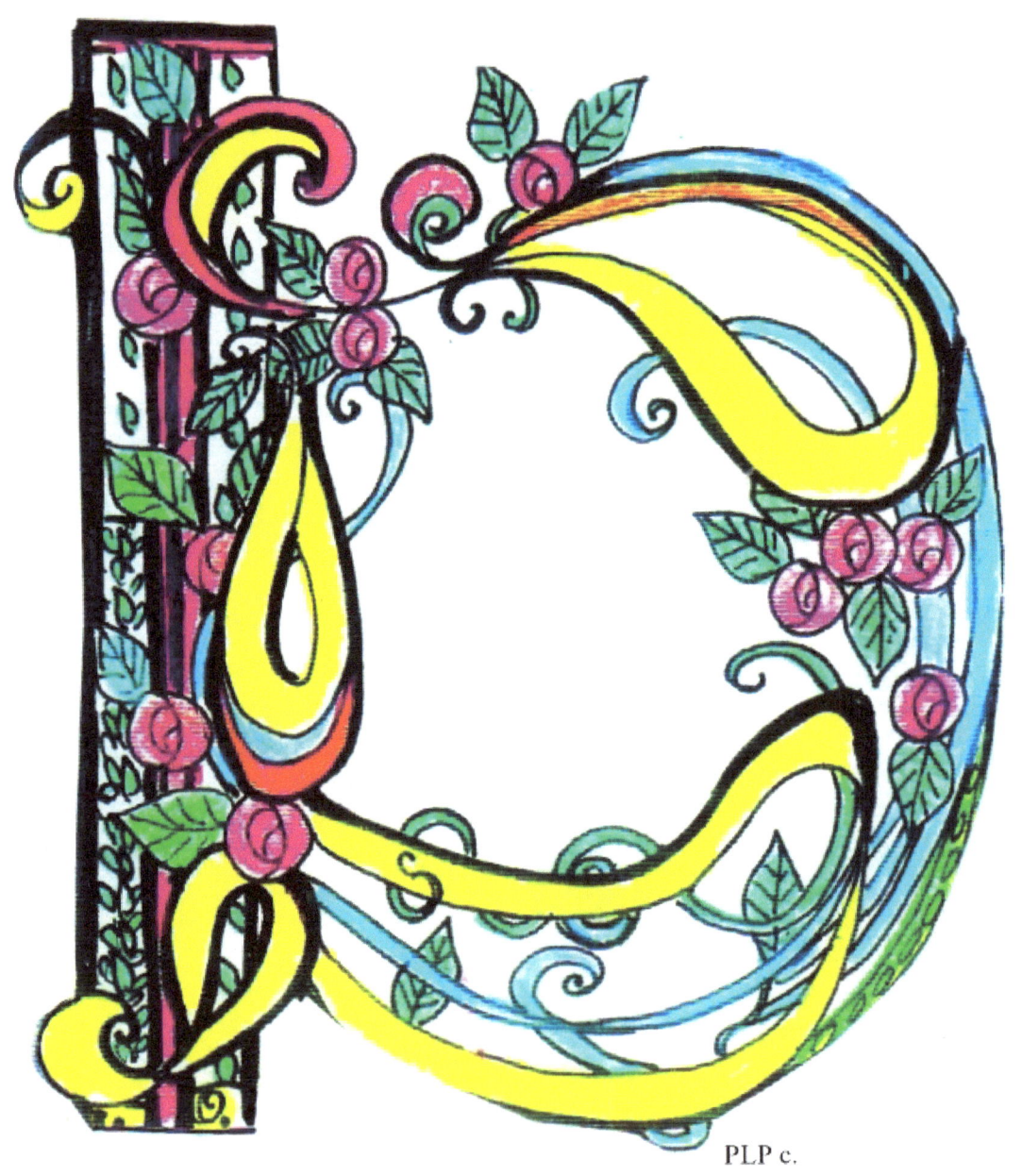

PLP c.

50

The letter D can become a beautiful beginning letter for a paragraph you are writing. It can be designed with one line or given thickness and great detail. Coloring it your own way and adding 3 dimensional add-ons gives it "your touch".

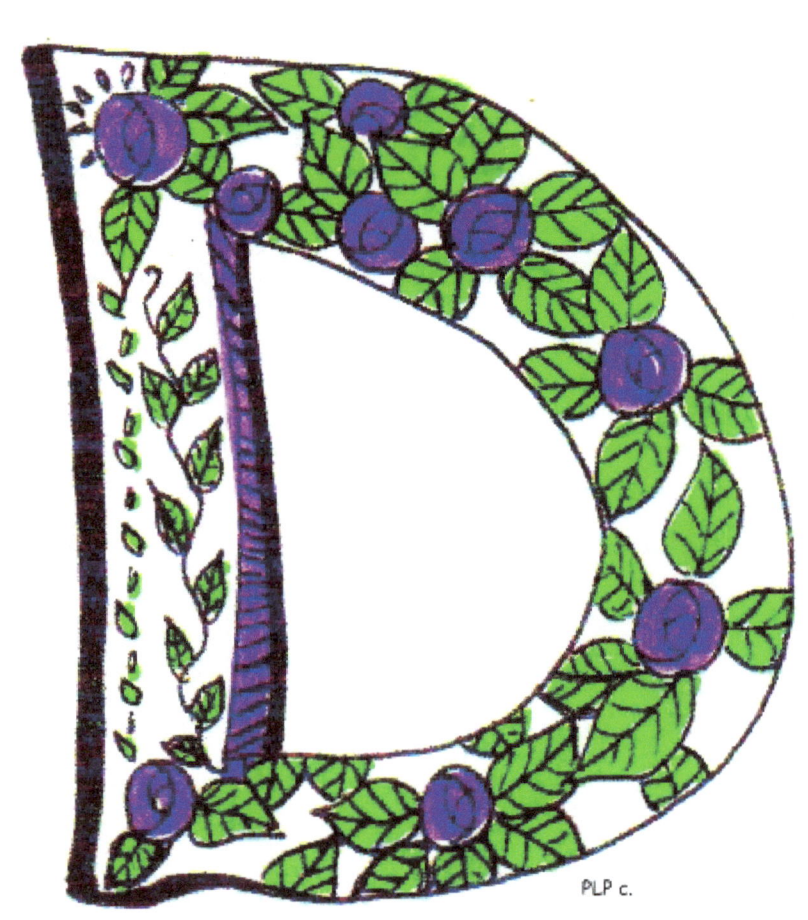

PLP c.

Maybe you would like to fill a big letter D with colors and flowers of your own.

PLP c.

Fill in the space with some kind of flowers with a pen or pencil. Then color them in with color.

Enjoy and celebrate the many possibilities with Letter D. Try some ideas of your own.

Can you find the next page in the black and white pages? How did you color yours?

If you enjoyed these pages there are books of other letters as well.

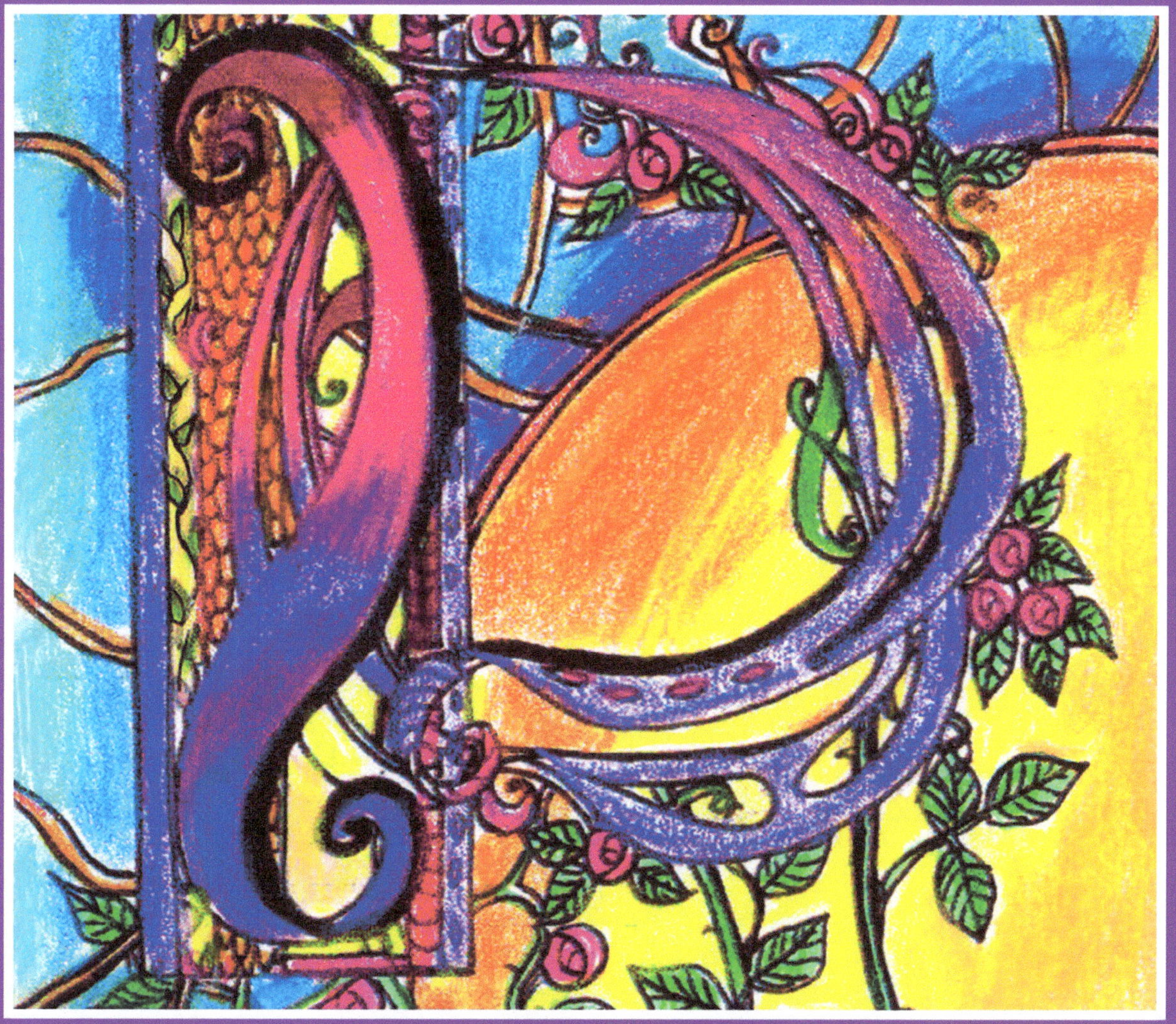

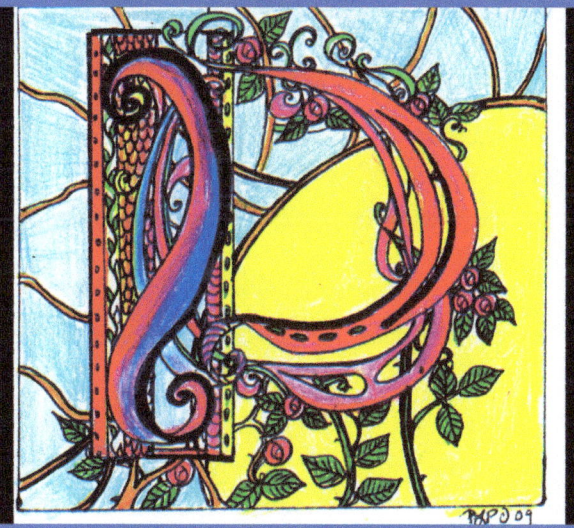
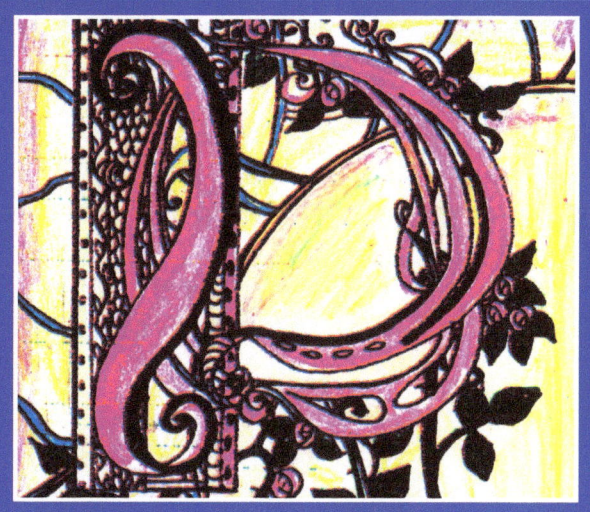

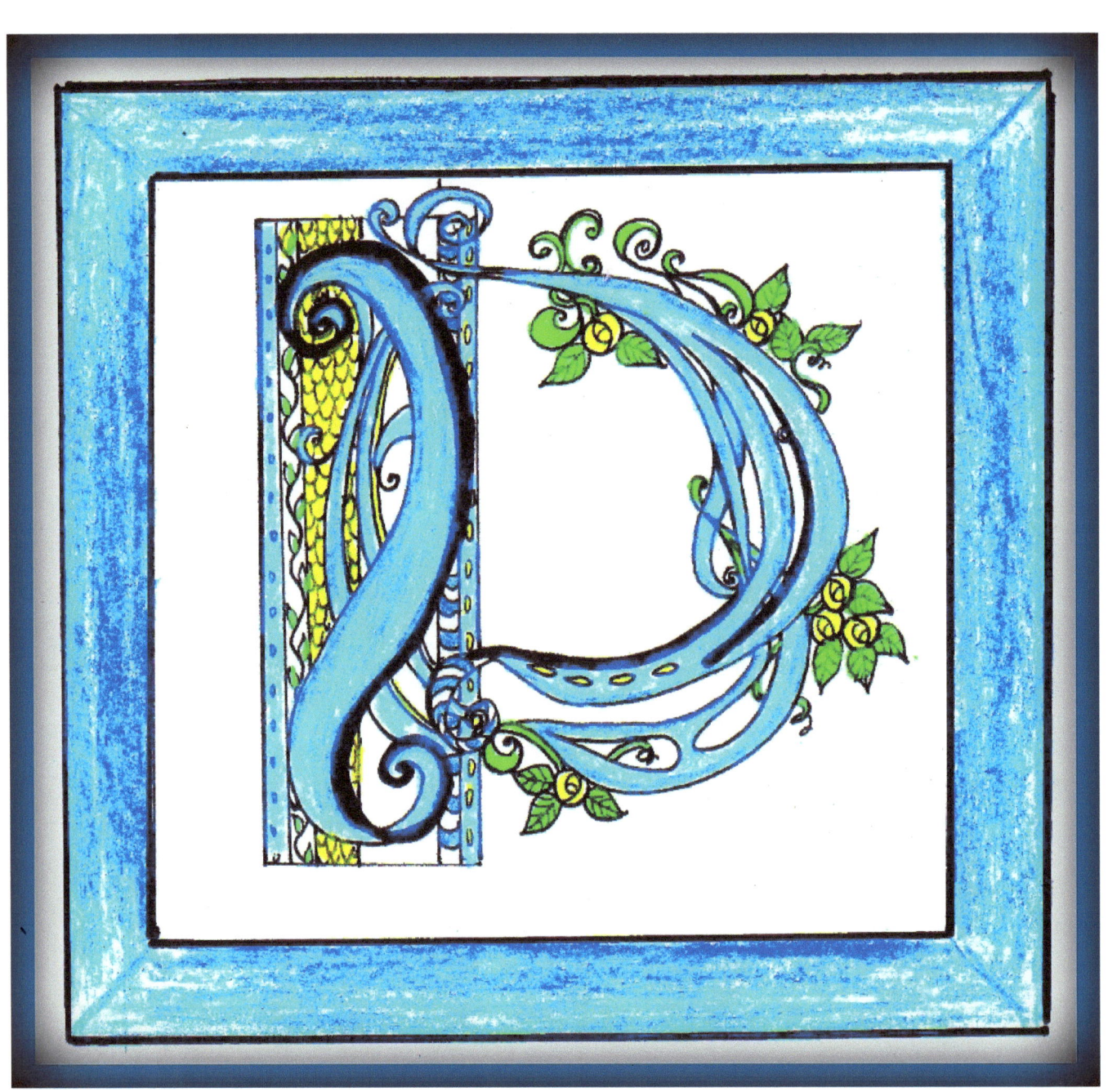

56

Hopefully you have enjoyed your letter D experience. My hope is that you will find ways I have not yet discovered to draw and color the Letter D.

Artist Peggy Louise Parrish